Instructions for Traveling West

Instructions for Traveling West

Poems

Joy Sullivan

THE DIAL PRESS
NEW YORK

Published in the United States by The Dial Press, an imprint of Random House, a division of Penguin Random House LLC, New York.

THE DIAL PRESS is a registered trademark and the colophon is a trademark of Penguin Random House LLC.

"Was It Always Like This?" was originally published in *Bracken* magazine (July 2020).

Library of Congress Cataloging-in-Publication Data
Names: Sullivan, Joy, author.
Title: Instructions for traveling west : poems / Joy Sullivan.
Description: New York : The Dial Press, 2024.
Identifiers: LCCN 2023038725 (print) | LCCN 2023038726 (ebook) |
ISBN 9780593597613 (trade paperback ; acid-free paper) |
ISBN 9780593729069 (ebook)
Subjects: LCGFT: Poetry.
Classification: LCC PS3619.U434 I57 2024 (print) |
LCC PS3619.U434 (ebook) | DDC 811/.6—dc23/eng/20231121
LC record available at https://lccn.loc.gov/2023038725
LC ebook record available at https://lccn.loc.gov/2023038726

Printed in Canada on acid-free paper

randomhousebooks.com

9 8 7 6 5 4 3 2

Book design by Ralph Fowler

For those who go.

Only now are we beginning to understand that all life on Earth depends on the freedom to move.

—Sir David Attenborough

I am the shore and the ocean, awaiting myself on both sides.

—Dejan Stojanović, *The Shape*

Contents

II.
Come Apart

III.
Commit to the Road

Interlude
Westward, a Woman Walks

IV.
Reacquaint Yourself with Desire

V.

Give Grief Her Own Lullaby

VI.
Remind Yourself, Joy Is Not a Trick

Instructions for Traveling West

First, you must realize you're homesick for all the lives
you're not living. Then, you must commit to the road
and the rising loneliness. To the sincere thrill of coming
apart. Divorce yourself from routine and control. Instead,
find a desert and fall in. Take the trail that promises a view.
Get lost. Break your toes. Bruise your knees. Keep going.
Watch a purple meadow quiver. Get still. Pet trail dogs.
Buy the hat. Run out of gas. Befriend strangers.
Knight yourself every morning for your newborn
courage. Give grief her own lullaby. Drink whisky beside
a hundred-year-old cactus. Honor everything. Pray
to something unnameable. Fall for someone impractical.
Reacquaint yourself with desire and all her slender hands.
Bear beauty for as long as you are able and if you spot
a sunning warbler glowing like a prism, remind yourself—
joy is not a trick.

I.
Realize You're Homesick

Remember What It Was Like to Be a Kid?

All skinned knees,
pavement and sick-sweet
candy in the sticky backseat.
How you stank of sweat,
bewilderment, popsicles, peppermint.
Swam in summer until it gobbled
you whole. Witnessed revelation,
trembling and silent: the rabbit's nest
between the stones, a dark bat winging,
the buck carcass at the edge of the wood
where you weren't allowed to linger,
and a woman calling you home.
How you found the jewel of language
and marveled at your wealth: *mule deer,*
blister beetle, blue ghost firefly. Each new name—
a little candle you brandished in the dark.

Long Division

My first friend was built like a willow tree. We were the same age but she was taller and leaner and impossibly graceful. *Hadessah* is the Hebrew name for *Esther*—the biblical beauty who saved her people from genocide. I was envious of her name and its heroism. Mine was *Joy*—flimsy and monosyllabic like *pond* or *soap* or *cheese*. Hadessah was smarter than me too, got better grades, and understood long division where all I saw was a thin bridge with numbers jumping off. But she laughed at everything I said and my god, I adored her. When you're little, love really knocks you out.

We said what kids say when you move. That we'd write. That we wouldn't forget. That, every night, we'd look up at that one weird winky star and make a wish. After she left, I could still see her bike leaning against the house, its blue body trembling in the rain.

Nothing is as lonely as childhood, and the person to finally interrupt that ache is a big miracle. You never forget the hero who slides into the bus seat beside you or scoots their tray over at the lunch table. The silhouette of someone small and familiar running down your street—sweaty and hopeful that *you* can come out to play. To this day, I can still hear Hadessah's voice at sunset. The bats winging in the dying light. She's calling out my dumb name. She's making it sound almost beautiful.

Late Bloomer

The bus aisle is a long series of choices. Above all, you want a window seat so you can fog your breath onto the glass. When no one is watching, you trace hearts.

You are, what teachers call, *a sensitive child*. Everything hurts. How other kids always shout in primary color instead of pastel. The way clothes seem to understand everyone else's body, but never yours. Once, you get your name written on the board for forgetting your homework. When the bell rings, you can barely stand. At noon, you find shame, Saran-wrapped in your lunchbox, next to the turkey sandwich.

In high school, no one asks you to prom and you lie on your back listening to records in the living room until your mother switches off the lights. You don't know yet that loneliness grows you a heart luminous as a luna moth, velvet, pea green. That all those days eating lunch in the bathroom will turn into poems. Days spent in the stands or as the understudy. All your intricate losses, your wrong nose and terror of locker rooms. These too will become metaphors. Every morning you watch the day seep through the blinds. Each hue passing through you: soft mauve, slow peach, muted gold.

Safe

For Tasha

watch out for the ice, i say.
be careful on the road, in the snow.

the fog, the rain. don't be sad.
please sleep. eat this arugula.
drink some water. wear your coat.
call me when you land.

there are a million ways to say *i love you*

& forgive me, i know nothing
about baseball, but something
in me breaks with joy when
the runner rushes in, body flung
& reaching, & the umpire
lifts his arms out like a prophet
or a mother & makes him *safe*.

Lemons

It was rainy season and everything in the grove was electric green.
I was hunting lemons. My job was to find the ripe among the
fallen. I remember the sweet stink of exhausted citrus. Spoiled
gold in the heat, how the fruit sweated in my palm. My sister was
running past. She was four years older, full of goodness and
gullibility whereas I was young and rotten and one for stories.
I used to tell her I'd seen fairies the size of tadpoles in the river.
That I knew a spell to repair lost time. Gullibility is a kind of
bigheartedness, I think, and when she finally learned the joke, it
always broke her heart.

Snakes were common in the grove, but I remember how horribly
beautiful this one was. How it lifted itself, an iridescent arrow.
Mambas are fast and deadly and when I screamed *snake*, my sister
stood among the fallen lemons, swaying slightly, weighing
whether or not to believe. I can still feel her eyes searching me,
the seconds slipping, the dying sun making her hair roar red. It
wasn't until I wept that she stepped out of the grove and for the
first time, I realized what words meant. I saw them clearly—full of
either venom or veracity. The dumb plum of my heart split open.
That night, I told my sister I loved her. I told her the truth.

Mangos

My mother was allergic to mangos.
Even peeling them made her throat thick
and her hands swell. I never understood
why she let me pull them from the tree
and carry them into the house. The fruit
sweating like lungs in my palm. My god,
she let me slice them in the kitchen, the air
sticky with scent. A form of love, I think—
how she'd stand in the doorway and watch
me eat. Juice on my chin. Finding the fleshy
heart. Sucking the pit.

(Luck I)

The last time I felt lucky was in fifth grade and my teacher was giving away a goldfish. She put all our names in a hat and miraculously drew mine. I was so excited, I cried. The fish only lived two weeks but, I loved him. It was years before I realized my teacher likely rigged the draw. Moments before, she had, in fact, whispered rather conspiratorially, that it just *might* be my lucky day. I was such a lonely kid and having a hell of a time adapting to the U.S. after living abroad and I think Mrs. Edelstein figured I could use a win. Of course the universe is full of deep magic, but I think most miracles can be traced back to someone's profound and quiet kindness.

Roads

Before Ohio and the roar of adolescence, my childhood was spent in Central African Republic. Because my parents were medical missionaries, I grew up transient and seeking movement, slow to root.

I remember how our jeep would rock down rust-colored roads, dodging potholes. I liked the jostle, the wobble, the glug of the motor. From the bed of the truck, I'd bump along, sunburnt and buggy. Behind us, the jungle, muscular, stinging with sound. Monkeys sailing from thorntree to thorntree. Kingfishers electric among the leaves.

My sisters and I would arrive home, caked with dust. As if God were baking with red flour and sneezed. How we'd rinse red from our dresses like blood in the days before we bled.

When we returned to Ohio, the roads were so sleek, they scared me. Car, mute on the pavement like the silence before a sob. No dust, no din. Only concrete and quiet.

Even now, I miss the sway and clang. I miss Africa, a continent I have no right to claim, a home I've no right to love. I feel pinched here, like a boot half a size too small—still trying to fit amidst a country that has no jungle, no sea of green, no monkeys shading beneath the porch or mangoes that ripen in my palm. No clouds big as empires or birds that catch the light like a flame. No roads that shake and return you baptized in heat. No dirt, the color of blood, that crawls into a belly and burns.

Mendelssohn

The neighbors kept a pet chimpanzee chained to the tree in their yard. His name was Mendelssohn, after the German composer, and he loved children. If we walked within range, Mendelssohn would pull us in, rock us like babies against his chest, his tremendous lips nibbling our lashes. He'd groom us for hours, belligerent with love. Leather palms and mango lullaby. Eyes tender as prunes. Untangling from Mendelssohn was the hard part. Touch-starved as he was, he couldn't bear to let us go, his embrace becoming panicked and painful. As he grew, we began to fear the strength of his sadness. He'd swing his arms out to us, but we'd only mournfully wave. Some nights, I imagined slipping into the yard. Unsnapping the collar from his lonely throat. Even now, I lie awake wondering if he'd have broken for the trees or reached for me. Given the chance, would he have hugged or run? Thirty years later, the question still squeezes me in half.

Buttercream

I was raised in a house that believed in the end times. By age 3,
I was convinced Jesus would return before my 4th birthday and I
wouldn't get my golden-haired Barbie and the chocolate cake
with tufts of buttercream. I bargained with God. I will be good.
I will *not* free the corn parrot from her cage. I will *not* wake my
mother during siesta. Delay your coming, Lord, just until after
the party. Heaven can't be as sweet as buttercream.

I grew up and the rapture never came. I shed God, or at least
tried, but I still found myself bargaining through the years. Let me
just have my first kiss. Let me just get into grad school. Let me
just meet the love of my life. Let me just see the ocean again.
These days, I don't fear God's return in a cloud of smoke and fire.
I don't pray. But when the love for this world gets too big and
achy inside me, I still catch myself begging—give us our kisses,
our fingers in the dirt, our sweat and our sweetness. Give us time.
Please, just a little longer in these bones.

Holy

My youth pastor used to drive us in a gray church van to the amusement park and all along those dark Ohio roads, he'd swerve to purposefully hit whatever crossed our path. Squirrels, raccoons, possums. Once, even a cat blinded by the lights. A velvet thump and the boys in the front seat weak with laughter. Later, on a dare, he swallowed a live goldfish in front of an entire gymnasium. It glimmered in his fist.

Before I learned Ohio and the odd cruelty of youth pastors, I'd been raised to give wild things berth and breath. To allow fire ants to march along their path undisturbed. Leave eggs untouched in the nest. Brake for baffled squirrels. Gently pry a chickadee from my cat's jaws. By age seven, I could pull a breeched puppy, wet and barely breathing, into my palm. Before first blood and baptism. Bruise and pews. Before fists. Before the brick of scripture. Before I knew who among us would be named holy.

Of Wildflowers

When I was young, I heard
So much about being
a child/woman/man of God
but then I grew up and all
I ever wanted
was to be of wildflowers,
of willow, toad, and bone.
of swallowtails, sow thistle
and cedar, of birds.

Gentleness

Today, I watched a young boy chasing a puppy with a runaway leash. The boy was frightened because the pup was close to the road and when he caught her, he hit the little dog hard and began hauling her home. The pup dangled above the sidewalk and I winced from the window. A man waiting for a delivery was also watching. He called out: *He's just a baby, right? He can't learn that way.* Soon, the man was setting down his packages and showing the boy how to hold the leash so it didn't pull. How to scoop up the pup and support his feet. How to talk firmly to a dog without raising your voice. Between them, a pocket of softness appeared on the street. Once interrupted, violence fell silent. I saw that boy carry gentleness home with both his hands.

Peaches

The nursing home stank of ammonia and loneliness.
Thirteen years with Parkinson's and still
my grandpa used to smile when I spooned peaches,
sticky with syrup, into his mouth. I was little
and my hand would tremble, the spoon would wobble,
my grandpa would shake, and my father wept
outside in the hallway. I never knew my grandfather
in the good years. Before the shaking
started and his memory faded but even now, I remember
climbing beside his pillow with peaches. He'd smile
when I appeared, and I think he almost knew
me then. *This is Joy!* They'd say and he'd stare at me until
he cried, swallowing slice after slice. It was good to see him
eat so I'd feed him them all and even after they were gone,
he'd still open his mouth. Recently, someone said my
grandfather never really cared for peaches, but he must've
loved the little hand that lifted the spoon. These days,
it's the world that topsy-turves. We all shake. Somewhere
in the fog, we beg holiness from one another
with an open mouth. We gulp, saying *yes, I love you*
Again. Again.

Geography Lessons

The first time I refused to sleep with a man,
he called my young body a *waste*
as in *wasteland*
as in the broken field where we buried the dog
the summer he got too frail to climb the stairs
or
as in the abandoned lot behind the burnt-out factory
where we rode our bikes and scraped our knees under
a sky as blue as god in the days before we learned
our bodies were a strange geography that men would try
to catch and claim and call their own as if our skin
were a lost country, a wilderness, a home built for everyone
but ourselves.

Growing Up

All I could think about
was filling these cups
and staining these lips
and being some new kind of loveable.
All the while, my mama in her quiet, weary way:
one day, you'll wish for this time without worry.
No one can really ever warn you
how the world is a thick leather boot.
A midnight car slowing down.
An oil spill. A matchstick.
I miss the girl my mother still could see —
unadorned, untired. The one, at dusk,
who followed the dog into the woods
unafraid.

Wind and Bread

When I was 14, my mother took me to pick out a purity ring.
It was an amethyst stone and the band, a bright gold clench.
There wasn't much of a sex talk. Instead, like Grimm's book of
fairy tales, I was offered a dark lesson. In marriage, sex was a
beautiful maiden. Outside it, a shrieking hag and shriveled ruin.

I was not yet familiar with the term *obsessive thought* or *post-
traumatic panic*. I didn't know how to fracture a story or upend a
myth or build a truth that didn't break you. So I worried and
smoldered and frenzied and somewhere along the way, my ring
came off. To my surprise, I didn't wither. I didn't witch or welt. In
the light, there I was—just skin and limbs and human stuff.

What curses us are rarely witches. Instead, it's the stories the
shape of someone else's fear. Shame doubled up in a big black
cloak. When I remember my girldom, I imagine Eve slipping out
of Eden. Running with no clear path, but she had lungs and wind
and bread. She had a river that pointed west. Above her, the
stubborn moon.

II.
Come Apart

Cost

Summer on the farm and under a June moon,
we'd sneak the mares out into the forest.
We weren't allowed to gallop, but no one
told the horses. In the dark, they seemed to sense
our blindness, our nervous bodies. Within
seconds, they hardly seemed the same creatures
that meandered on trail rides, bore children
in the ring, the horses we named Sugar
and Jelly Bean and Dumpling but in the dark,
they morphed out of shape—splitting like a river
among the trees, our reins loose and useless,
and in those moments, we couldn't scream
or steer or stop. We were something new then,
a part of them, swimming in the air, suspended between
stars and trees and hooves and horse sweat. Swallowed
in a tide we couldn't escape until finally, at the sight
of stables, the horses would soften and slow. Spell broken,
they'd gentle back into quieter animals. Ones that ambled
to the stall. Amenable to apple slices
and nose scratches, kerosene lamps making
their shadows long, and we'd dismount, silent
and sober to discover what it cost them to carry us
back into the light.

Mercy

Once, we were grilling zucchini
from the garden. It was summertime
and I was about to leave you.
A praying mantis landed on the grill.
He was bright and beautiful
even as he fizzled and I burned
all my fingertips trying to save him.
You can't tell when an insect is in pain
but he must have been and you put him
in the grass so softly
where I found and stomped him.
And I think it surprised us
what we each defined as mercy.

Exodus

my heart's gone out of it,
I say, and what I mean is,
it left the house cold,
barefoot, and probably
in the rain. It was a Sunday.
There was no note.
It simply wandered out,
in a sheer gingham dress,
in search of someone else.

(Luck II)

The woman at the park says:
lucky you
left when you did.
Her mouth—
a wine-red oracle:
better to carry
an empty suitcase,
than a suitcase
with a scorpion inside.

Wood Frog

The day I found out my partner had relapsed. I was in California.
The sky so blue, it howled. I'd just eaten a lemon strudel and put
honey in my tea, stacking pleasure upon pleasure. That morning,
we'd sent each other love texts, the sexy kind that make other
people blush.

Here's life: one day, you're planning a wedding and the next
you're packing a suitcase and gambling how far half a tank can
take you. You're stopping off at bars to flirt with men in tall boots
and stupid haircuts. You're shifting sideways on the sidewalk to
step over a pile of ants, wishing just once some god would decide
not to squash *you*. You're writing poems and drinking whisky and
bleeding all over the driver's seat as you miscarry your little
dream.

Is there a way to love and not die? I'm not sure but the Alaskan
wood frog freezes solid in winter only to blast back in spring. Give
me that story—the one where her little toad heart, after months of
chill, switches back on. Tell me again how she quivers and thumps
and shudders awake. Again, how she thaws and opens and out
croaks her summer song.

Velveteen

Ricky was a stuffed raccoon with red fur and a black button snout. Two chestnut eyes, loveworn and peeling. I took him everywhere, his long torso flung over my shoulder. With that secret suspicion present in all children, I believed the thing I loved was alive.

I thought that if I kissed Ricky's eyes enough times, it might shake him from slumber. That he might wake and witness the breathing world. In preparation, I pocketed whole eggs, hagberries, bits of cheese to feed him. When the magic finally came, I'd be ready. Over and over, I kissed his face and his plastic eyes paled.

But miracles are a funny, fickle business. They tip over without warning. The boy at the end of the road lived through winter, but his sister did not. A rainbow's end appeared, ripe and watery in the backyard and I slipped my hands into it but felt only air. Once, we went outside and watched dumbstruck as the moon moved in front of the sun. With all the universe's strange and unsteady miracles, how is it possible that love can't start a heart?

The day you relapsed, I wobbled out. World spinning on its delicate hook. I packed my things in silence. After all these years, I'm still a woman without miracles. No magic in her hands. If I had but one, I'd set down my suitcase. Fool, a final time, I'd swallow you in my arms. Lift you over my shoulder. I'd find your face, kiss your eyes. I'd make you live.

State of Emergency

We never guessed how much we'd miss
the hot and sticky hugs and standing close
enough to whisper. Glory of reach and grasp,
nudge, nuzzle, spoon and squeeze.

I've heard the phenomenon is called *skin starvation*
and it's the reason infants are laid naked
on their mother's breast the moment after birth.
Because touch is how we greet one
another in almost every language and say: *you are here
and I am with you and we are not alone.*

I confess I've not yet learned how to translate
the gorgeous shock of seeing you. Even from 6 feet,
I wonder if you can feel the electricity of my skin,
pining in its sweat song, so helpless and hungry:
hello hello hello.

After, We Try to Switch
Our Hearts Back On

There are no mountains in Ohio so, on Sundays, I take my heart
out for a drive. We speed a little. I rush the hills fast so I feel them
in my throat. Later, I let someone kiss my mouth. Brandi Carlile's
voice breaks on the record player and I buy all the strawberries I
can find because they are furious and red and beautiful. In the
evening, we dance around the kitchen—dogs shaking off rain. I
wear a little black dress for the first time in 8 months. My heart
cracks like an egg. The world spins so loudly now. In the
swimming pool, the checkout line, the middle of the street, I want
to ask—is it over? Are we different? What happens now?

Singing Whale Unmasks New Giant Blue Whale Species Hidden in Indian Ocean

(Headline in Forbes, *Dec 29, 2020)*

Scientists called it *a composition of moans, snores, and chirps,* and I think about how, this year, we had to discover new ways to hear our hearts. At first, that bellow ballad probably sounded a lot like moans and cries and sobs until suddenly we were dusting off forgotten guitars or gliding down the street on creaky skates. Pressing flowers and making art, writing poems and baking sourdough, planting gardens and then pickling our darling little vegetables.

The truth is, creatures can either create or shrink. We've finally had time to listen to who we are—to that person who previously got buried beneath business trips and traffic jams and crowded malls in that blaring din they call *normal life* and whether or not you are a great blue whale at the bottom of the ocean, in this year's slow and merciless stillness, I hope you found a way to sing.

In the Office

We wear thin armor, as if approaching war.
During a meeting, a man explains
why his ideas are good, perhaps brilliant.
The days rifle past, full of paper cuts, nerves,
and filing cabinets. The copier, a monstrosity,
glares in the corner and waits to break. In the lobby,
there is enough sugar to kill a horse. At the company
party, the receptionist gets drunk and begins
to weep. We sneak our joy in slices—
on holidays and weekends, sandwiched
between calendars and PTO.
Vacations smear at the edges. Traffic eats us
like ants. *Work-life balance*, someone
says. Outside, our lives ring, unanswered.

Tiger Farm

A tiger cub on a tiger farm
wakes to find his explosive
body, fire stripes, crocodile
eyes, the whole of him beginning
to be huge. And he won't know
why his paws are the size
of river stones or why his teeth fang
in the jaw. He's only ever seen
the metal gate flimsy on its hinge,
hurricane fence, a scrap
of sky. It doesn't puzzle him
how his slaughter arrives
limp and beaten, to his massive
maw, but he's growing and growing
and feeling the pinch. In dreams,
he senses it, same as you,
that beyond the compound, the cubicle,
the chain link and headless chickens,
there must exist something, somewhere
wild as grass, so cool and soft
beneath the paw.

Submit

On Fridays, a pop-up from my long-dead work calendar appears on my dashboard—a leftover from the days I worked in an office. Like the Ghost of Corporate Job Past, it simply says *SUBMIT TIMESHEET*. It's the last digital artifact of a time when hours fell in neat, numeric rows. Columned, clear, infinite.

I don't actually know how to delete the recurring notification, but even if I did, I like being reminded of the life I've left. Reminded that no flashy title or hard-won promotion compares to the sensation of my hand out the window or rush of pines turning against twilight. The stars overhead, bright as bees in the night's dark mouth.

Recently, my parents visited me in Oregon and I watched my father kick off his shoes and wade into the sea for the first time in forty years. For decades, his work kept him from the water. I'll never forget how he submitted himself to the waves. How the ocean rose to meet his old body, after all this time, as if she'd been homesick for him.

Giving Notice

One day soon, you'll rise from your desk or quietly excuse yourself
from the meeting or turn the car around in the middle of the street.
Anything might trigger it. An open window. A sunny day in April.
Daffodils panting in a mason jar. Call it madness. Call it glorious

disappearance. Call it locomotion. Do what you should have done
years ago. Let your body out to pasture. Fill your calendar with
nothing but sky. Surrender to the woods. To cicadas and sap
beetles. To the moths, the color of memory and dream. Wear
dusk like an ancient cloak. Hurry—

there's still time to *creature*—to pluck all the wild cloudberries
and carry them home. Even now, you can hear coyotes crying
at the canyon's edge. Find your first fang. Grow back your hackles
and howl. This was always your chorus, the mother tongue, a feral
hymn you know by heart.

III.
Commit to the Road

Howl

This morning, the sunshine is thick enough to swim
in—as if you could fling yourself into it and float.
I want to wear it like a robe. Squeeze it into my suitcase.
Swallow it whole like a hot lemon. I am finally a woman
willing to feed herself—light, bread, joy. Sometimes,
you don't know that you're starving until you've had
a proper meal. That's when your heart really begins
to howl—when it learns what it's been missing.

Teeth

The dog used to disappear, sometimes for days, into the woods.
Once a stray, she never seemed to quite shake it. We'd watch her
run—her slim body evaporating into the mist. Eventually, she'd
materialize again—all mud, moon, and dried blood. Rib and
limp. Someday, she wouldn't return and we knew it. This was the
deal she'd struck with us. The cost of loving a wild thing. These
days, it's my stray heart panting beneath an April sky. I've taken to
hiding out in cabins on weekends, road trip after road trip, bare
feet in the open field. Something tugs me with its teeth. Peels me
from the life I've built—the one with a blue house on the corner
of the street and people I love on the porch holding mugs of tea. I
can't stop thinking of that dog on the edge of her wildness. How
she knew she was about to leave her home, her girl, her warm
corner of the bed. Even still, the moment she stretched beyond
the property line, she sprang for those dark pines like she was
born for them. She leapt without looking back.

Leap

Nothing my friends tell me shocks me anymore. No wild dream or *unadvisable plan* or moonshot idea. Recently, my friend told me she wants to move to Wyoming to be closer to horses. She tells me horses can hear your heartbeat from 4 feet away. That's enough for me.

Another friend is relocating to Peru. Another to Alaska in search of his true north. Another is adopting a child. Another is turning down a killer job so she can finish the book she's been trying to write for years. Another is leaving the man of her dreams for a woman.

Look, America is awful and the earth is too hot and the truth of the matter is we're all up against the clock. It makes everything simple and urgent: there's only time to turn toward what you truly love. There's only time to leap.

Ghost Heart

What do you call nostalgia for all the places
you'll never name *home* as you roll through city
after city with its old brick and swoon of field
and sky. What is the term for all the futures
unhooked from your chest and slipping back
into the lake like a fish too beautiful to cook?
Can you grow a ghost heart like a phantom limb?
Does it thump at the sight of a stranger turning
slightly as if he heard you say his name?

At the Airport

Everyone's a little high
on love or grief. All of us moving
toward or away from something
we want. Imagine the million
intimacies security must witness
as thousands of passengers shuffle
past in socks. TSA, a priesthood
ushering us forth. Imagine
their bemusement at our unholy
elements: our pill bottles and vibrators,
anti-itch cream and pink mouth
guards. Phone chargers and tampons,
mint floss and exhausted earplugs. Histories
hobbled together, secrets askew, a whole life
collapsed into a suitcase that we push blindly
through the birth canal of a baggage scanner
before turning to ask: *are we good to go?*

(Luck III)

I somehow got upgraded on my flight today to see my family and because I'm almost never lucky, I'm trying to be very quiet about it. The attendants even gave me free whisky at noon which is definitely a mistake but also one I'm going to make because it's free and for the first time in a while, something nice and not horrible has happened. Also, if not for the grace of strangers who let me cut them in a holiday check-in line that lasted for centuries, I most certainly would have missed my flight. Now, I'm in premium class drinking whisky and worried if anyone is nice to me, I'll sob.

A woman on Instagram once posted about the fact that she gets upgraded on flights all the time because she's able to manifest luxury and the universe loves her like a *little spoiled brat* and god, I can't relate. I am decidedly *not* the universe's spoiled brat. I'm no one's petit chou. I'm the universe's weird great-aunt. The one drinking whisky and writing poems in the bathroom and swiping left on Bumble and running for her flight—terrified she won't get home for Christmas. The thirty-something woman who is just trying to get there—wherever *there* is.

The Cashier at the Gas Station
Asks Where I'm From

And when I say Ohio, he says *Go Buckeyes*
which I understand as a stranger making an offering
of language that can be shared. The way starlings
roost on a power line, scooching over
so the other can sit, flocked and fanning
feathers against rain and never in my life
have I seen a football game, but still I reply
Go Buckeyes
which is a way of saying: I accept.
I would root with you in imaginary stands.
Cheer at the same time in a darkened bar.
We are more alike than not, us two.
Here, let me shift, shuffle. Shelter a moment
beneath this wing.

These Days People Are Really Selling Me on California

where no one yet has broken my heart. When I left Ohio,
I left backroads and the endless chop of green

meadow, the cicadas roaring in the splintered heat.
At a party, someone says: *Oh, Ohio I spent a summer*

there and now we have this in common: a corn moon
hovering over a harvest. Mulberries sinning red against

the inside of the mouth. I would like to touch the world
and not harm it. I would like to be touched and not

harmed. A friend of mine growing up on a farm
found her hair in the nests of robins. Dark strands

in the structure of the cradle. This is a compliment
I would like to receive. A synonym for purpose.

This must be how a fledgling defines holiness. How
the air gives back grief. Make me something made of flight.

Yearn

When I was only a few years old, I disappeared. For hours, my mother searched the house, the yard, the palm trees swaying with early grief. I imagine how she must have screamed to her god, turning silent in his sky-bed. How my sisters must have run to scour the street.

I don't remember crossing the road, sagging with traffic, or arriving at the beach but what my neighbor found at the ocean was indeed me—a toddler thigh-deep in an eddy. I'm told he lifted me from the waves wet and unrepentant. Baptized by my own hand.

Nor do I remember being carried home, sopping to my mother's arms. From a distance, it appeared I'd drowned and somewhere in my sternum, I can still hear how my mother wailed. How she keened between rage and relief, besotted and terrifying. A monster of love. How I was spanked, then cradled and cloistered for days.

What I do remember:

The gallop of waves and light. Brine stinging the air. How the ocean lifted herself through my open window and ached me outside. How I only wanted the wet and when I reached the water, the tide buried itself in the best of me. Its salt-ghost haunting the edge of all my new language. Inside me now, even now, an ever-whispering tide.

Move to Oregon in July

And you can drive to the coast and slurp oysters from the shell in cafes with tiny brass forks and fancy chilled plates. Or you can pass a lavender farm and feel the scent creep through your skin and into your dreams. Soon, you'll be ordering brandy manhattans at the bar and trying on names like Clementine or Genevieve. Maybe even Ava if the bartender seems sad. A one-eared cat might follow you home. Loneliness is a bright blue dress with an open back. That's the way of it, isn't it? One day you're sitting alone at the bakery and the next, you're standing across from the ocean and the next, you're crying at the movies and after that, you're planting fruit trees and learning street names and bringing in the mail and kissing someone's delicate face. You suddenly realize you've slung together something called a life. The word *home* drops out of your mouth like a ripe summer pear plopping in the backyard. Sticky at the edges. Heavy with sweetness.

January

First winter in Oregon, it rains so much
I drown like a slug on the pavement. Damp
to the bone. Soaked beneath the socket, the groin,
the armpit. Yesterday, I was out hunting poems
in the garden. Scouring the doom, the glowering,
the goldenrod. Looking for a metaphor that wasn't
wet. Lately, only dark mud, sullen pigeons. Little slog
and wise decay. Everyone rants about the rain, but my
neighbor has lived in Portland for 30 years. She wilted
in California before the dryness drove her north. As long
as it rains, she says, anything can be new.

Interlude
Westward, a Woman Walks

Hunger Pangs

I was raised on scripture, sharp as an eyetooth. For years, I felt those verses like a dull ache in the jaw. A fever burn. After Sunday school, it was my job to gather the leftover flannelgraph from the board. Wilted piles of Bible characters with saturated color and fine lines. Wrinkles around the eyes. Quietly, I'd stack the soft scenes like a tailor arranging fabric. A girl sorting.

Once, our teacher told us the story of Genesis, but she got it wrong. She listed the days of creation out of order. Land before water. Frogs before birds. I knew but didn't say a word. We all went home and had supper. *Any story can crack*, I thought. I chewed around the eyetooth.

Of all the flannelgraph figures, I liked Eve most. I liked the arch of her brow and her red mouth. In Hebrew, Eve means literally "to breathe" and she did, indeed, seem a warm and living thing. When the teacher wasn't looking, I'd face Eve westward out of her garden and roam the animals out of rank. I'd scatter the trees. In my hands, Eve didn't just pick apples, she gathered papayas, persimmons, mangos, rambutan. She wore a mouth of yearning. Young as I was, I had the wisdom to fill her palms with fruit. I knew enough to let her eat.

He Called Her

And Adam called his wife's name Eve; because she was the mother of all living.

He called her *sky* first. After the ochre light that shimmied into morning, but her soul was too big. So he called her *star* since she reveled like a galaxy. Soon, she bellowed and shook and birthed. Something stars cannot do at all. So he called her *creature, blood, orgasm, quake.* This was not right either. Finally, he called her Eve, because she was alive. Because she made everything around her alive. And because to him, the name sounded like rain falling. Like the click of crickets. Like the soft hum of your mother's hands folded over a lump of dough, the sensation of her palms summoning the yeast to rise.

Hiss

Eve loved the way the snake could twist and strike. She loved his speckles and thick shine. The way he could sway his neck in the air like a song.

Adam had named everything in the garden. From the clouds to the dolphins to her own hips that curved like a conch shell. But Adam had not yet seen the snake, so Eve called him what she liked.

In the deep heart of the afternoon, she sang with his head curled against her chest, his body coiled through her crimson hair, a beautiful forked tongue resting in the last unnamed part of her body—the notch at the base of her humming throat.

Storm

Eve couldn't leave Adam because Adam was the only man on earth.

This significantly lessened her options.

She also couldn't leave him because they shared a rib.
If they strayed too far from one another, her left side
began to moan, as if to warn of rain.

Adam couldn't leave Eve because she was the only woman on earth.
She *was* his earth. But even if she weren't, Adam couldn't leave Eve
because she was the only thing that ever made him
wail or roar or lust or laugh

until his one lonely rib ached in his throbbing chest.

Feast

Fruit after fruit, Eve feasted. Lemons drenched in summer, blackberries dark with dusk. She grew watermelons as large as her sons' heads, and mothered banana trees until their bright buttery children rested in her palm.

She chased God in every taste.

A bite of strawberry could send her straight to Machu Picchu. Once, after a kumquat, she found herself in New York City, where the air swarmed with noise.

Eve had no words for what she witnessed. She simply swallowed and saw.

Sometimes, in the future, she spotted God or perhaps something *like* God. Once, in a pasture in France, she stumbled upon what looked like a pale version of her maker. He was a tall man asleep in the grass. Eve searched his wrinkles for recognition. When she found none, she left him softly, sending him something pleasant to dream of.

Inside Eden, Eve had been a berry. Unbruised, but unripe. Now, she was a woman barefoot at the edge of the earth. At night, she lay awake with her boys pressed like pods against her and thought: *Love is the only garden worth dying in.*

What Eve Knew

The exact hue of the sky, I imagine,
and the size of light, how it empties
into everything. How to live, I reckon.
After the fire and the angel, after the earth
began to disintegrate beneath her weight.
When the grass broke underfoot—
how to not leave your body.

I imagine Eve knew where to bury
a sigh. What to do when Adam
clouded over into anger. Why, out of all
the languages of the universe, rain
is the one worth listening to.

Maybe she learned where memory goes.
Why dirt is the first and last and best
thing we touch. How to cradle hope
and death in the same fist or test fruit
without leaving a bruise.

I would like to ask her so many things:
how to rub shame out of your best blouse
how to survive a bee storm
how to be a storm
how to make God storm
how to survive God.

And as God Had Promised, They Became Mortal

When Adam saw his wife, he loved the shape
of her—imperfect, slightly sagging. He wanted
to cup her in his hands and kiss her dimpled thighs.
Adam found wrinkles in his pockets and freckles
in his shoes. Eve laughed and wiry white hairs sprang
from her head like garter snakes. They savored time
because it was running out.

The earth went wild and the harvest hungry.
Babies came and Eve foraged muskmelon,
sweet corn, plums the size of conch shells.
Leaves shed from trees and the sky changed
seasons like a ball gown. The ocean stood.
Mountains were born.

Adam and Eve tired and discovered sleep. Soon,
dreams were invented. They dreamt they were little
gods, mouths full of fruit. They dreamt
they'd never die.

When Eve's last tooth fell out, she wrapped it
in papaya leaves and presented it to Adam.
Until his dying day, it was his favorite gift.

Eve's Apology

Lamentably, my apology is serving a life sentence and
cannot receive visitors. To be honest, my apology just
bloomed into a field of scarlet peonies. I plucked them
into a bouquet that bled all over your breakfast table. My
apology is stuck in traffic. The weatherman predicted a
storm of apologies next week. However, until then, it will
be sunny. My apology is on its period and the cramps are
really bad. Sadly, I've recently gone apology free. Don't
put any on my sandwich. Unfortunately, I've shaved my
apology and we'll have to wait for it to grow back.
My apology has a dentist appointment. Excuse me,
I misspoke—my apology actually just burst into flames.
Truth be told, you just missed my apology. It left through
the back door. Check the bar. Thank you for your inquiry,
but my apology is currently out of the office until forever.
I regret to inform you that I have killed my apology
by wringing its neck with both my hands. Don't worry,
it didn't suffer.

A Trick

Eve stood sheltering the goats from rain.
They had survived their first winter,
and spring was its own wet beast.

No one had seen God in centuries.
Eve missed his songs, his clumsy dancing,
the way he could make fish leap

like a laugh. In the early days,
she had pulled light from the air
and taught God to rainbow it

from one end of the earth and back.
It was a trick he could not forget.
Eve longed for what was. Before

the garden and God's departure,
before the thunderstorms
and Cain's banishment. Before

heartbreak ripped open the horizon.
Eve had one pleasure left: the flesh
of fruit. Again and again, she bit

and broke free. A billion years later,
I was in the airport staring at the little birds
pressed against glass, the ones mottled

by windows, dumb things, seeking light
in lieu of sky, when, I saw her:

a woman
in a dark suit passing
my gate. She didn't see me,
yet I knew her by the half-bitten
mango that shimmered in her fist.

Eden

He said: If you leave me, I'll go hungry.
Above them the moon paled and held

its breath. She said: Come with me;
it will be easy in the dark.

He said: It isn't the right time.
She said: I'm one hundred years old,

and I'm tired. The grass began to slither.
He said: The crops will fail,

the animals run wild. She said:
My body will be the harvest.

She flexed the sentence like a muscle.
The tree panted and sighed.
He said: I'm afraid. She made a web
out of her hands and caught

his face. She said: I'll go first.

IV.
Reacquaint Yourself with Desire

Want

They say men want freedom
and girls want love,
but I've seen women leave
lovers and countries and kingdoms
of comfort just for the chance
to sleep unbothered, to bathe
unwatched, to waltz around
apartments all their own,
wearing nothing but lipstick
the color of desire.

Solo

There is, of course, the delight of dining alone—
a single candle and dedicated bread basket. Tiny
butter rose. The particular pleasure of sunsets
secretly witnessed, coffee sipped silently,
poetry read in private. The delight of walking home
after dark when the air is full of heat and insects
and then, the joy
of traveling by yourself—reading Didion on the train,
swimming nude or snoring, eating peaches
from the can, arriving late but wearing red shoes.
Of smoking solo off a balcony overlooking a bistro—
the French one playing *Rhapsody in Blue*.
The patio full of mustaches and strangers
and lemon cakes covered in scandalous amounts
of glaze.

[lˈəʊn wˈʊmən]

If you google the phrase *lone woman*,
Thesaurus.com provides the following
synonyms:

spinster, prig, old maid, goody-goody.

Live a year in your own bones
& learn alternatives:

sequoia, jig, open meadow, good, good.

Red

Once on vacation, my mother, for lack of sunscreen,
smeared her lipstick on my lips and sent me up the mountain.
After, she did not make me rub it off, and I felt

red throb me through. Ever since, I've been drawn
to that particular hue. What you might
call candy apple or fire engine or summer tomato.

Slap-you-on-the-cheek red. Rob-you-blind red. I've learned
how red is a verb—the way eyeliner is a weapon. Red makes
a party of any outfit. Red requires delicacy. It stains

and smears and sweats. Conjures the color of moon cycle
and blood, hot pepper and smut. It can ruin

a man's collar if he isn't careful because red spreads.
When my therapist asks me about desire, I think how
men muss red from my mouth like a little victory. How I leave
it on wine glasses and teacups as a calling card. How I want
to wear red, smoke red, drink red. Eat and dance and sleep red.
Cradle red, bathe red, rage red, weep red.

Why Read Poetry
if It Won't Make You Rich?

For starters, your soul will get bigger.
Your love, more terrible and luminous.
Soon, you'll say tender things at parties
after too much champagne. A sidewalk
quince, wet with midnight, will stop
you in your tracks. In time, you'll
find the perfect metaphor for your
child's face. All at once, you'll see
the world and want it again:
clothes flapping on the line,
lilacs strewn and seeding, the luck
of worms. An artichoke with its heart
torn hot and steaming from the throbbing
crown will suddenly turn you on.

All Day Long There Is a Bursting

Give us, we ask, our daily bread. But soon, we crave
the sweet. So many books, yet the child screams for candy.

Summer is stumbling out of season. Autumn aches in,
the wild gold of its moon ripening, our secrets hot inside us.

Look, how even the bee begs the honeycomb.
Mouth, an oval of need. We long to name the yearn.

The unflinching joy of saying: I want this.
To touch each other and say: I want this.

A taste of honey: I want *this*.

My Friend Tells Me She
Thinks of Flowers During Sex

Their dark eyes and tiny ovaries and throats
the shape of bells. She imagines them all
different ways: soaked in a rainstorm, wild
in a field, mussed, nibbled, strewn. Moth
orchids really send her. Not to mention
tulips who get sleepy
and tuck themselves in at night.
Or begonias that tremble at the touch
of wild bees and thunder. The world is full of men,
but my friend is a botanist. Her desire is in details:
carpal, drupelet, scent. Blossoms that mother
into fruit. Each pistil, a dart of dreaming.
Each petal—a soft lip searching.
Each stem, a staunch body, singing
like the rest of us
of the dirt from whence it came.

An Octopus Has
Three Whole Hearts

and sometimes I lie awake thinking
about all that lub-dubbing
on the ocean floor and no one to hear it.
What kind of god gives a cephalopod
three but a human only one?
I want more thumps. I want more time.
I want to waste my love on everything.
Give me a heart for Ohio. Another
for a silk butter moon. Another
for the park bench man who swoons
for doves, his quiet hands full of crumbs.

I Haven't Prayed in Years

I haven't prayed in years
but if I did start
I would never say the word *please*
because if you're praying
then, well, that's implied.

And I would never say the word
dear because that is too formal
like a thank-you card to your grandmother
that your mother made you write
after you got the ugly ornament
that one Christmas when you were ten
and you still have it because throwing
it away now somehow feels like cheating.

I would never swear in a prayer
because that seems risky and if
you are praying, you generally aren't
feeling ballsy. You are all out of balls
and that's why you are praying.

I'd never write down a prayer either
because written prayers are sort of like flags
in that you can't burn or rip them
up so you bury them and then
are secretly disappointed when
nothing grows out of the ground.

I think if I started praying
I'd put bees inside
that prayer so it buzzed in my mouth
and fell off my tongue and into the air
thick and swarming, a hot cloud
that could sting and sweat and swab
like honey.

I'd put a matchbox in my prayer
so I could make a fire and if
God didn't hear the prayer
at least he'd see the smoke.

(Luck IV)

Luck, like any little deity, is deeply mysterious and rather unknowable. Best to treat her with only reverence and gratitude. We don't earn luck and she certainly doesn't owe us anything. Manifestation talk stresses me out because it usually means someone is trying to sell you something. Or they want to make you feel bad for being uncertain, where, in reality, uncertainty is actually a beautiful posture of humility, in my opinion. The truth is—we're all distant relatives to the stars. We're bizarre cosmic improbabilities and the most astounding luck is that we're here at all. Listen, I don't know if we make our own fortune or if we're given it. I don't know if karma is real or if we attract, magnetize, manifest or whatnot, but here's some unconfirmed science I live by: love is a really wild energy and like any force field, the more you send out, the bigger the boomerang.

My Mother Says Kissing a Man Without a Mustache Is Like Eating Eggs Without Salt

Which is a better way of saying—take the scenic route. Say *I love you* when it's true. Drive 12 hours just to touch. Buy kumquats because they're called *kumquats*. Call someone you love a little *kumquat*. Write letters. Recite poems. Be verklempt. Rise early to hunt the moon. Eat pastries whose names you can't pronounce. Astonish everyone. Haunt everything. Sing, even if poorly. Press the peel for zest. We're nothing but brief bodies. Hearts, fragile as parakeets. Spit, lips, and longing. All we've got is this skin. This necessary salt.

After Covid

I'm still only smelling the fringes of things: lemon cusp, garlic echo, lip of lavender. Whiff and ghostdream. Shape but no body. Smell therapy tells you to sniff a strong fragrance for 20 seconds and imagine the scent, encouraging neural pathways to forage meaning. Scientists suggest vanilla, thyme, tangerine. Bergamot or jasmine. But when I imagine a life without scent, those aren't the ones I miss.

I miss the reek of gasoline and loneliness. Pew seats stale from heat. Smell of chlorine and childhood. Mint gum and sunburns. Salmon withering on sand. Give me havoc. Give me funk. Rank of horses, spent and frowsy. Manure on boots. Borscht on stove. Give me malt, brine, vinegar. Cedar of my grandmother's attic. Insects winging too close to campfire. Good god, give me your shirts, sweatier than sin. Come to me ripe and rare. Unperfumed and pungent. Love-stenched, gamey, merciless.

Save your rosemary and gardenia. I'll take the skunk of it: musty books and animal breath. I want the wet dog, decaying garbage and apple rot. Life, give me your stinking mouth. Bend, let me kiss it.

Blue

I've taken every man I've loved out
for oysters especially if he's never tried them.
It's hard to explain how eating oysters
isn't so much about taste but about the memory
of ocean and brine, wet crag and sputter-foam.
How you lift the shell and slurp wave, sargassum,
primordial star. Suddenly, the ancient rush
of dune and tide. Lungs full of froth.
How you quiver like a drowned god
and swallow that gulp of sea, creature made
of salt and time and I am asking to be loved
like that—with a taste so blue it breaks you.

Sockeye

Bizarre that we met in the slim bar at the end of my street. How seconds before, I'd pinched my cheeks to make them pink. The way the night shot off like a hot-blooded horse. Each muscle of evening working us closer, tying our bodies in a sturdy knot.

I like men from Alaska. When a person is surrounded by silence, it softens something.

In time, you peel the day off me. Your face close to my face. Awkward and funny—the frankness of it, how our mouths insist on one another. Two rivers that likely never would have crossed, for an instant, splitting ordinary time.

After, you talk about the salmon caught in summer's late rage. Crowds of them pulsing the shore. How they sometimes spit the shining hook. That they are named after the Latin *salmo* which means *to leap*. This is a fact I did not know and I feel it in my spine like a lucky shock. Our bellies hot with laughter. Better, I think, than being touched or even loved, is this—reaching, leaping toward what flashes in the sun. The life that is briefly ours.

Comment Section

Today, someone is angry with me for writing a poem about eating oysters. I don't tell her that oysters lack a central nervous system and likely feel no pain. I don't tell her how I have so many food sensitivities, I run out of things to eat. I don't say I'm tired.

Yesterday, someone was angry because I don't know if I believe in God. Someone is angry that I wrote the word *tit*. Someone is angry that I had an orgasm and then wrote the word *orgasm*. Someone is now likely angry to learn that some women have tits and orgasms and gods that allow them pleasure.

Someone tells me my teeth are crooked. Someone writes me that their mother is dead. Someone tells me I should want children. Someone messages me that the planet is dying as if I did not cry about it at midnight standing in my underwear outside on my deck in the dark. Someone tells me I should be sorry. Someone DMs me that I am sexy. Someone says they want to write poems just like me.

Almonds

An Uber driver recently told me I'd be a good mother. I think it's because I involuntarily screamed when we almost h t a squirrel. That or I have the hips for it. The truth is, I don't know if I'd be a good mother. I worry that I love poetry too much. And sleep. And Paris. And how, right now, my body is still just my body—with no one else's footprint.

I heard once that ovaries are the size of almonds. Sometimes, when I see a man cradling a child, my almonds quiver. I imagine someone small of my own. I want to show her what a prism does after it swallows light. I want to feed her pears.

The thing about babies is that they're so *irreve*-*sible*. Tiny monsters of need. Each, a wound of love. Every day, I wrestle with the desire to give a child this world and an ever stronger urge to save one from it.

My friend says biology is a bitch, which if you rhetorically analyze long enough—is so true, it hurts. Look up the word and there, on the page, you'll find the standard definition: a female dog, wolf, or fox. Read between the lines and you'll spot also—a woman, aching.

The Electrician Sings
"Easy Love" in the Kitchen
While Fixing My Light

Sea ice around Antarctica reaches a record low
and now, on the news, a man rushes down the streets
of Kyiv, his toddler in his arms. The word *war* enters
every room. Earth warms. In Texas, a child grows
bright with grief. Everything threatens to burst.

In the morning, my belly asks again for a baby.
I leak with longing. No one has told my body
yet about the world. All she hears is the sound
of someone in the other room,

still singing.

Gatsby

I used to call him *Gatsby*, which made him tilt back in his chair
and laugh. Once, he took me up in his plane and rolled down all
the windows so I could feel clouds. I swooned for what his lovers
had all fallen for: vintage cars, pinot noir, perceived tenderness.
Tweed jackets and elbow patches. Keats on the coffee table. The
day I discovered he was married, I took myself to the nearest park
and lay in the grass until dark. I finally found pictures online: a
wife. Two daughters. He offered no apologies. His wife knew but
wouldn't divorce him. Why shouldn't he have what he liked? The
world was made for men like him, he said. One day, he'd move
out west, drive along the ocean. We never spoke again.

Last I heard of Gatsby, his wife had, in fact, left him.
The womanizing never stopped. Once, someone spotted him
trailing down Main Street drinking wine from the bottle.

Turns out, it's me who moved west. Me who drives to the ocean
now so I can feel salt in my throat. Recently, I noticed Gatsby's
ex-wife started following me online. I doubt she knows who I am,
but she likes my poems. I'd like to walk with her on an Oregon
beach. Sun on our skin. Sand in our armpits. Maybe we'd talk
about the men who mark us. Or about the new world she's
building for her daughters. I want to tell her I'm building it with
her. I'd like to stand close for a moment. Twin fires from a
distance. Before us, the furious sea.

Horse Girl

Recently, I discovered that for approximately the same amount I pay a fitness coach to tell me how many calories to eat monthly, I could lease a horse at a nearby farm and ride whenever I like. This realization was both hilarious and sad. Either pay someone to dictate your carbs or gallop an Arabian stallion through the wood, your newly resurrected heart racing like a wild rabbit beneath your blouse.

I've always been afraid to admit I love horses. Growing up, I worried I'd be labeled a *horse girl*. More than just being kind of weird, I knew that *horse girl* meant something worse. It meant that you loved too much. That you loved wrong.

But I can't help loving horses. I love their huge dark eyes and terrifying nostrils and exaggerated lashes. I love the stink of them, slick with mud and creature sweat. How the scent of hay and dung sticks to your skin. How it exhausts every muscle in your thighs just to stay on.

Yesterday, I got to meet my new horse. I got to bring him carrots and feel his enormous lips on my flat palm. There are two ways to love this world: in nibbles and snatches, throwing glances over your shoulder. And then there is this kind: loving off-script, hot-blooded and mammalian, bodied, muscular, with your ribs aching. The kind of love that makes you offer your heart up— plump and flushed. Love that asks to eat you whole.

V.
Give Grief Her Own Lullaby

Sister

Let me come and weep beside you. Here
now, give me your knots. Let me take
your bitter bite & honey it. Let me
say *oh* as you unravel your ache.
Let me walk beside you in the heavy dark.
Let me put my lantern out as well
so we can sit together in the blessed black.
We will be so still. Let me take your child
in my arms, & let me lift her up also.

Brother

for the man who followed me down the street late at night whistling.

Brother, I see you, a sting beneath your tongue. Look, inside your palm is a snake rattle, the shed skin of cobra. We've left the garden. I've shed my long hair. You forget that the moon is my grandmother who watches you with her skeleton keys. Let's meet up, brother, in the next life. When you are a woman walking alone down a dark street. When you are holding a key sharp-side-up. You'll hear a whistle, a low rustle, a slither. See how light always eats the darkness clean.

My Mother Asks How I'm Doing with Just Whisky and Cats

None of us were built for this, after all.
Loneliness enters the house and takes
off her boots. The days lose light.
I keep hoping for the postman —
his everyday footsteps, a kind of friendliness.
There is no name for this kind of breaking.
It's November and my neighbor sets off fireworks.
The moon is an aching white eye. Some nights,
I sleep inside your old shirt. Even wolves need
a soft body to curl toward in the dark.

Duck

When you were little, you had a tiny
glass mallard named *Love*. You carried
it in a soft fist. Once, the duck slipped
and fell but didn't break. This made you
believe in the impossible. Later, you would throw
Love against the wall. You were young and touching
power. When the neck cracked off, you put
Love's pieces beneath your tongue and tasted grief.
That was the year you learned anything can break:
A glass duck. A young tooth. A human heart.

Before

Soon, you'll rise from a bed you won't make. You'll go downstairs. Cut potatoes into cubes, crack eggs, reach for salt. Next comes rain and work calls. The hot engine of day begins.

But for now, shadows are still pressed thick against the window. Morning is here but hasn't been announced. Grief has yet to spot you, though you hear her hunting. No one, yet, has spoiled the dark by singing. The air outside too cold, even for birds.

Dream

At night, I dream of holding
everyone I have ever known:
the cruel cheerleader from 9th grade,
the boy who left me on the dance floor,
the bus driver, the postman, the professor
who once, in workshop, made me weep.

In my arms in my dreams,
is the sheepdog from our childhood farm,
my mother and her trembling hands,
the man who paints the house next door
the darkest shade of blue.

(Luck V)

Because tonight, the clouds rolled
out their pink crinolines and lingered
until dark. Because when my sister
called, we did not argue. Because
I saw the squirrel and braked in time,
and when I made a joke, Sara
laughed. Because they sprayed
the lawn with poison but the cat
went around and because I slept
and was swallowed in the mercy
of dreams. Because when grief came,
as I knew she would, she only soft-pawed
up the gray carpet steps and stood
in the doorframe, watching
with her yellow eyes.

Burn

The waitress at the highway diner calls me little mama. I like that, even though I'll probably never be anyone's mama. She's closing up, but says I can stay and write awhile.

The man who cooked my steelhead has strong hands and a loud laugh. He lingers at my table. After dinner, he walks me to the parking lot, carrying logs from the kitchen as I'd been asking after firewood. He doesn't let me pay and soon, I'm watching him split the logs beside my car. He's handsome in the way grief makes strangers desirable. It's so cold beside the sea. Soon, he is telling me how to make a fire with your hands. Three sticks, an open damper, burn the cardboard box if you need to. What fire needs is air, he says. It just has to find a way to breathe.

As Women Do

On my hike, I forget about daylight savings, misjudge sunset, and
find myself running for nearly an hour against swiftly approaching
night. I'm not much of a runner usually, but it turns out I'm fast
in the forest after sundown, gambling my odds against a man or a
mountain lion. Halfway through my run, I bump into an older
woman. She's facing the ocean and spins almost as if expecting
me. A brief acknowledgment, then we're silent again. Still and
watching the sea. Overhead, the stars salt into existence and we
finally turn to walk each other to the park lot. A quiet agreement
forming between us in the shared language of lanterns. Making
light, making steady, making safe. As women do.

Bonus Parent

Inside, you are warming up leftovers for the kids and organizing their shoes. I spot you from the quiet of my car, soft and secret like a glimpse of deer in the pocket of the wood. I can hardly believe I'm about to drive away from this—the shared calendar, the soccer games, chore chart, the microwave. The way your children do not yet know how to introduce me to teachers. How they simply say: *this is my Joy.*

Separate

On Tuesdays, I revisit the life I could have lived. The house I tried to home. The children who were almost my children. I sit at the dinner table with my ex. Peas on the plate. We look away.

The child who isn't mine is in the doorway waiting to share a book. It's an old one about a secret wall and a magic door. I've tried to tell him 3 times that his dad and I have split. That the future is now full of doors I won't walk through. Each time, he changes the subject. Look at this picture, he says scrambling for art on the fridge. I try again. He scoops the cat and shows me her paws. I try a final time. He holds up his elbow and shows me a scar shaped like a tiny star: *Look*.

Sad Museum

Don't write just write the sad, you say. *We are not a sad museum.*
Remember the good: the cabin at Rainier. The hike up Shasta
Mountain. The night we ate mushrooms and got slaphappy, then
slapsad and wept at the sight of wild pears. Not to mention all
those mornings, faces flushed across pillows. Hundreds of
perfectly runny eggs. Hot showers and slow putting on of shoes.
Car rides, knees touching, kiss-kiss and *don't be late.*

The night we turned in the dark and took each other like a bride.
Your tongue, a messenger of light. How can I explain? Some
stories are so soft, they sting.

The way we once found a grouse nesting in the woods. A break in
camouflage and suddenly, there she was, her belly burdened by
eggs. Her secret speckles and exposed white throat. She was so
beautiful, it was unbearable. We kept walking. We pretended we
didn't see.

Men Ask Me on Dates
During a Global Catastrophe

Would you like to walk around the park in the dying light?
Would you like to have a drink on the patio?
Would you like to not talk about despair?
Would you like to Zoom?
Would you like to FaceTime?
Would you like to Google Meet?
Would you like to spend the night?
It's the end of time, after all.
Would you like to ask me about my childhood?
Would you like to make me laugh?
Would you look at this world?
Would you still like to try and fall in love?
Would you like to hold me through winter?
Would you like to weep?

Was It Always Like This?

The way we pay attention now. A fat red tomato asleep in the
garden. The neighbor boy offering me his last stick of gum. Wine
straight from the bottle. Grief that shelters in our throats.
Showering, a ritual unto itself. Bird calls that nibble us awake.
The altar of our palms. Shielding strangers with space. Dancing
when we'd rather sleep. Sunshine so bright it invents the lost word
between holiness and magic. The way we wash the vegetables
these days, so *carefully*—as if cradling a child.

Lucy's Papa

A professor and his 9-year-old daughter, Lucy, live beside me. After school, Lucy scratches my cat's head and tells him he's *a magnificent boy*. She recounts embarrassing stories about her papa, where the best hiking trails are, how to outrun a bear. A library of little facts.

Yesterday, I read the climate report. More accurately, I skimmed it. Grief is better borne in bite-size portions. Someone told me once that tree roots cuddle in a forest fire. We should all be screaming. My gynecologist says there's still time to freeze my eggs. I calculate how old my baby would be in 2050. I calculate how long the atmosphere can hold. Beyond that, I don't speculate. *Remember, grief — bite-size.*

This morning, Lucy's papa shows her how to stake a tent carefully so the sides don't lean in. Their tent is the color of an olive moth. I've never heard him raise his voice. Together, they lay out the rods, puzzling the best way to pitch. According to Lucy, there are only 7,500 different species of butterflies left on the planet. Everything slides toward despair. Except Lucy's papa. He's too busy pulling the tent up on rails. He's working quickly now — hoisting the shelter, asking her to brace. He's unzipping the roof flap, gathering up what's left of the light.

Balloon

Just this morning, a farmer pulled white
balloons from her pasture where her sheep
had grazed on plastic. Working the rubber
between their round sheep teeth. Latex sticking,
like syrup, in a lamb's warm belly.

In the mountains, they find bighorns too,
ribbons bright in their gut. It isn't just sheep
but the screech owl, the dolphins and whales
and turtles, the rusty seabirds that catch
on our corners. A sparrow sliced
on a coke bottle. The way the sky is littered
with human joy. How glitter gluts a fish.

It's difficult to be alive and full
of sharp edges. When I started this,
I was trying to write a funny poem.

William Shatner in Outer Space

*"When William Shatner returned to Earth, on Wednesday morning,
from a four-minute sojourn into space aboard a Blue Origin rocket,
he appeared genuinely and profoundly moved."*

—The New Yorker, *Oct 2021*

When William Shatner looked down, he wept like a cracked god.
His grief, the size of Mercury—silvered and hungry. The curve of
earth appearing poignant as a woman's pelvis. What weightless
William saw was a planet impossible and spun, unhinged in a
galaxy, a speck imbued with blue, shock of language fraying at the
seams. Wave world, the dolphin chorus, whale flank and beetle
heat, Sahara and coral reef teeming with grief. Gorillas and
penguins and blue-tongue frogs, the bafflement of snails. History
measured out in thimbles. What William witnessed was your life
and mine. A small blue flame.

Sea Salp

There you were—a clear blob on the beach
quivering like a prayer. When I saw you, I pierced
you with my walking stick. The startle
of your body, slick with slime-sap, running.
At first, I thought you a bubble or algae. Later,
Google said you're a salp or sea grape—
a tiny ocean invertebrate with no spine to speak of, but still
a brain, a heart, a row of dots that work as guts. Forgive me
for not knowing that a group of you is called
a *bloom*, that your body shimmers beneath boats
and sometimes shields smaller fish from sharks. Everything
is in service to something. Even me who is reckless
and slow to learn. I google again, this time:
what to do when you harm an unarmed creature
washed up and resting. What to do when something
brief and necessary bursts.

When My Friend Is Low,
We Walk by the River

It's somehow still a pandemic and we have nowhere
to put our rage. My friend tells me how he has begun
to imagine the finishing touches of his life. He counts
the things he's lost. As he talks, I imagine tethering
a silver thread from his body to mine.
It's dusk. The geese are all headed home. Our two bright
shadows grow longer. Grief is a clump of dark feathers
in the grass. The sky runs purple and petals cut.
We look around. It's almost cruel, he laughs.
After everything, how the world still *insists*
on being beautiful.

Pushing the Belly

When you meet the beluga of your grief
in the open ocean, do not pierce or pet it.
Do not ride or tame it.
Do not feed it anything other than yourself.
Instead, let it roll you in its mouth,
mold you with its gargantuan tongue.

Let it swallow you whole.

Arrive like Jonah in the soft underbelly of lament,
in the whale of your own sorrow, drown.
Settle among the tattered fish, the carnage,
the fishermen's hooks carved into bones of rust.
Push your hands into the raucous heart,
feel it beat wildly against your palms.

Begin to crawl.

Up the colossal throat and past monoliths of teeth,
climb out like a hymn. Rise like a stupid miracle
flung upon some sun-fragrant rock,
shocked and land-hungry, wet with whale spit and resolve.
Cup your hands to your heart—full now with the sonar
of sadness. Remember how it propelled you,
breathless, towards the shore.

VI.

Remind Yourself, Joy Is Not a Trick

Seed

When I was 27 years old, my left tit began to bleed.
Straight from the nipple. As if I were lactating blood.
The doctor said my tumor was the size of a sesame seed—
which sounded innocuous, but we knew better.
Breast cancer runs in my family. I had to wait 6 weeks
to discover whether or not that seed could kill me.

For 42 days, I asked the earth if I was dying.
She always answered the same way—with clouds
and wet tulips. Birds in the early movement of morning
A heap of newborn stars.

My father wept on the phone, but in the waiting room,
a stranger with a shaved head held my face. My surgeon,
a precise and merciful woman, left me without a scar.
My tumor was benign, but I wasn't really the same.
When the pandemic hit, I moved to Oregon to be closer
to the mountains. Joan Didion died and I booked a trip to see
the redwoods. I quit my job and now, I write late into the night.
Sometimes, into morning. I avoid work that feels meaningless.
I call my friends. I thank my body, though she breaks. I kiss
my lover in public. Often, I go out walking, even in the rain.

Anointing

Just now, someone is shaking
the branches of cherry blossoms
onto the heads of children.
The rose bushes berserk
with beauty. At the intersection,
a man yields, waves pedestrians
through like a priest. Everything purrs
with oncoming heat. Green is a new
language the whole city learns
as if even the trees are trying to translate:
bless, bless.

Raze

Every March, they'd burn
the withered brush behind
our home and we'd watch
flames slap the trees. Ash
like worrisome snow. We
stood small and clean in
an ocean of heat, close
enough to witness wild things
with singed paws. To see what
leapt from earth's most private
places. Birds flushed from nest,
civets strange in sunlight,
gazelle flung far from hidden
thicket. Fire is a hard lesson
but listen, whatever in you has been
burnt, sunk, or shot from the soft
chapel of your chest,
swept from its animal home
and stranded in unbearable soot—
learn what we did when the rains came
and wept. After every charred ending,
green always heels round and doubles
back. Life lurches in.

When the Queen Dies

The wisdom
of bodies and of bees
is to rebuild. It is to enter into

urgency & draw breath.
It is to begin & rename,
an old wound suturing

the comb. Listen.
Feel the scars that sleep
silent on your body, how

the skin wrinkles into prayer.
Tell me—who was the first
voice who told you

about brokenness?
Who whispered
that your soul's monarch
was dead? Even then,
which parts did you siphon
into honey?

When All This Ends,
I'll Throw a Party

where everyone gets a kiss.
i'll cradle your face like a baby.
we'll drink bourbon from the bottle
& eat berries from the garden.
we'll gloriously sweat, romp & revel.
no one will be shy.
we'll whisper & shout until the last
of our loneliness leaves. we'll dance
under a fat lemon moon & when
the song ends, we'll forget
to let go.

Open Mic

We were sitting quietly and waiting to read when a woman cut
her poem short and began to shake. At first, I thought *seizure*
and nearly stood until I saw the torque of her body lifting, beginning
to shimmer. How language took her in an unbearable wave,
drawing her limbs up, not like a dance, but like a lustrous god,
a religion with no apostasy. Her shoulders trembled, mouth open
and quaking, an animal in heavy rain. This is a poem isn't it? Isn't it?
My cheeks were wet. The shape of her, a question building for which
I knew I had no answer. Watching her was like making love
or slipping on ice or being born. You hit the hard edge of the whoosh
and are ushered into something new. A ground bird tossed into the sky
for the first time *up up up* as if finally in flight.

The Telescope

I was still a young girl when my father took his long-throated telescope out of the study and sturdied it toward the night sky. In those days, we lived far from the city and when evening came, it didn't creep, but surged. A canopy of darkness. A herd of stars.

There was only one man in our town who had never seen the galaxy up close. When he was called, he approached as if arriving at an altar. He bent, shy, eye to canister. Before him, the sudden sky.

I would give anything to see the world just once the way he did—fresh and for the first time, newly smashed with joy. To roar with that kind of shine, hands outstretched. How he peeled back, silent and shaking, and began to laugh. Such a sound—as if he'd swallowed the splendor of that light and it shone back up through his open mouth.

Instinct

I've heard elephants think we're cute but I doubt it.
Instead, it's humans who are easily charmed. A species
delighted by yellowing leaves and the decency of dogs.
We're tender mammals mostly. Trying to keep each other afloat.
Scooting earthworms off the sidewalk. Scooping our hearts out—
like oysters from the shell. A kink in evolution's engine maybe
how we marvel at meteors. How my mother brings in daffodils
to rescue them from frost. Even I know a sunset doesn't save us
but still I swerve to the side of 405 just to see the sky squish pink
beneath night's dark thumb. Is it defect or advantage—this impulse
to cradle what is soft and small and never truly ours? This instinct
beyond sex or survival—a genetic code that interprets mountains
as something holy. The moon as wonder. That spots a shaky fawn
in the dew-slick dawn and roots for it to live.

Litany

When people wave to each other at the park.
When toddlers wear overalls and dogs roll by in strollers
even though it's dumb. When the woman at the gym,
between very heavy sets, tells me today is her rat's 1 year
birthday and she's having a party. When I see people teaching
each other how to change their oil. When you melt into my palm
when we talk about your mother. How your breath smells like love.
When men say goodbye to my cat. When people sleep in waiting
rooms so they don't have to separate. When my nephew wins
at Uno. When anyone puts their hand outside the car window
and into the wind.

I Took My Body Out to Dinner

I opened the door for her. Draped the linen napkin
across her lap. Fed her sauteed mushrooms licked
with lemon. Bought her a second glass of wine:
darling, you look lovely tonight.

When it was time for home, I said I'd like
to take her out again. The rain came and I covered
her head. In the bedroom mirror, I asked forgiveness
for letting men love her when I could not. Patted the ripe
pillows of her thighs. Her ostentatious ass. Marveled
at the good dip of her belly, softness of her breast,
sweet wizardry of her feet.

I stood in awe of her beautiful bones.
I begged her not to leave me.

On Days I Hate My Body, I Remember Redwoods

Give me more time on earth, and I'd take
any *body*. A body ripe or ruined. Monstrous
or errant. Make me a redwood tree.
Body becoming branch becoming sky
becoming breath. Make me a slug upon
her neck. The moth wilting at her roots.

I don't want a heavenly body, but a body
of dung and dirt. A bruise-able body.
Any form the shape of yearn. Give me fur
and snout. Hunger and burn. Bone, fin
or wing. All I need is a heart for breaking.
Just a mouth to open

     and taste the rain.

Queen

Years ago, a pregnant stray cat showed up in my backyard. She just crawled under the fence one day with a belly full of kittens and hunger. Her need was urgent and simple: she wanted relief.

At the time, I was acutely aware of my proximity to the title of *crazy cat lady*—that insult we hurl at women who find themselves husbandless past the age of 30. I'd just kicked my boyfriend out after he got drunk and aggressive. Now, I was feeding cats.

At Target, you can buy a Crazy Cat Lady starter kit for only $19.99. The toy figure is dressed in slippers and a nightgown, plastic hair adorned in a crown of curlers. She comes with seven cats and a face full of wrinkles. This world loves to sneer at women in all their ugly mercy. Even so, I took mama cat in. I let her have those raging wet babies on the bathroom floor. I gathered the bloodied newspaper. I buried her one dead. Mama's ears were chewed from frost. She had a mouth full of cracked teeth. We both bolted at the sound of a man's boot on the stoop. She showed me her scars softly—the way women, over too much wine or perhaps not enough, flash their pain at one another like a flare from a dark island.

Language is often unforgiving. A merciful woman is deemed mad. A dog in heat is termed a bitch. A female possum is a jill. But sometimes, semantics get it right. Did you know the name for a mama cat slipping into the summer straw, her peach-sized belly swollen with blessing? Her—they call a *queen*.

Soup

I'm sick and my ex brings me a thermometer, cough syrup and
Gatorade, six cans of Campbell's chicken noodle, and my favorite
popcorn.

He leaves it on the porch and stands a ways off, waiting for me to
come down. Me, who feels like a possum in a dumpster—feverish
and barefoot, unwashed hair, holey sweater, red eyes. When I see
him, I make a joke about dying. The moon is nearly out. The
street between us, wet and shining. He waves and says: *I love you*
so softly I nearly miss it. It lands on my coat as I turn to go inside.
All my life, I never really thought I deserved love, yet here it is,
clinging to me like sweat.

FaceTime

Now, my ex and I call each other to say the kind of *I love you*
which has slipped into something hard to explain. An odd
perfunctory kind of devotion reserved for lovers who no longer
make love.

He drives while we FaceTime. Growing a ponytail and talking
about his new relationship which makes me dense with relief.
The connection stutters. We stumble over our words. Always an
echo between us. Jitter and latency. For a moment we're frozen,
the pair of us, stilted and blurred, a half step behind one
another—smiling but missing the other. All I can hear is his voice
saying: *hey, can you hear me? I'm still here.*

Old Habits

I wiped out on my bike yesterday. My ex was with me and helped
me up and it was romantic for a moment in the way romcoms are
romantic when the love interest leaps to the rescue in the
wounded aftermath and gently dabs their lover's lip and fixes
them up with bandaids and kisses: *oh, this might sting a little*.
Except that this is real life and he spills hydrogen peroxide all
over the couch as he tries to bathe my bloody elbow and my torn
up knee and I'm crying but not in a sexy way and we're not lovers
anymore but still there's love. Not the fireworks kind, but the
familiar and sweaty and honest type that carries you home and
slaps a bag of frozen broccoli on your bruised thigh and
accidentally calls you *baby* again—as if you might not notice. As
if your heart doesn't thump like the tail of an old hound at the
sound of her name.

Sad Lovers

Years ago, I fell in love. Not with the man that I love now and who is likely reading this over his morning coffee, eyebrows gently raised. My lover now is the kind of person who picks me up at the airport and packs me lunches and rubs my feet. But before him was an artist who didn't do any of that. He'd only whisk through town long enough to break my heart. He was, what my mother would call, *a handsome devil*, more devil than handsome. Craggy like driftwood. Easily swept away.

I wanted him in that way we want what will wound us. Heart hellbent on what will strangle it, run it over with a taxi, leave it ramshackled in the woods. He used to come to my apartment, make a mess of all my books, between us—two bottles of wine. He loved women, but never only one. Never *completely*. I can still see him draped across a window seat, the front stoop, my lap. A danseur and I, his sad ballet. In time, we dwindled. Flames eaten by rain.

I spent my 20s on men like this. Poets with drinking problems. Musicians who brought guitars to parties. Depressed devils who'd spill melancholy all over my best blouse. Then with the gift of my 30s, I got tired. Tired of holding up men's sadness like a bent trophy. Weary of men with deep wounds and an aversion to therapy. Exhausted by men who set the table but never asked me to sit.

Here's what I know: nothing, not even sad lovers, is as beautiful as the ocean in October. Or the summit of St. Helens after you have heaved yourself up five miles of volcanic ash. Or the feeling of wading in an Oregon hot spring so naked you could spit. Someday, you'll stop yearning for lovers and their mournful eyes and sharp edges. You'll know how to build your own fire in a cold forest. You'll find yourself in the middle of life's wet howl and you'll recognize what a bright thing you are. You'll reach for only what will burn you back.

(Luck VI)

Looking back, it's a blessing we didn't
buy the house—the one with marble
counters & a merciless green lawn.
Lucky I never marched down the aisle
exclaiming: *the happiest day of my life.*

Fortuitous—the missed flight to France,
the Thursday I bled through my best
dress, how disaster lit us like an exit sign.
Bless the arguments & the venom.

The straw that broke our backs & the chapel
that never saw us wed. Bless the body of our love
that could not breed. That lived & died—
a strange creature, more end
than beginning, more myth than fact,
more crow than dove. A dark bird, bless it,
that never found its wings.

If I Had a Hundred Lives to Live

One of them would be on the side of the mountain with sheep
and a speckled doe. I'd hunt eggs each morning, knit sweaters
made of wool. Or, I'd be a man in New York, thighs on the
subway spread like a little god. Learn to move through the world
without flinching. Or maybe I'd marry myself to a piano, play
tunes on the second floor of a townhouse in Prague. Watch all my
neighbors dance. Maybe I'd write a book about moonglades or
master the soufflé. See opera at the Teatro Colón. Pluck foxgloves
on the Western Cape. Or maybe,

I'd hurry back to this life, the one where you are standing beside
the open window looking drowsy and beautiful, a half-eaten pear
in your left hand. *What?* You ask, handing me the other half while
we silently watch the rain.

Tomatoes

I waited so long for love
and suddenly, here it is
standing in the garden, hands full
of heirlooms hot from the sun.

Soon, we'll make a supper of them.
Salted slabs between slices of bread.
Your beard silvers. My hips ripen.
The mail piles up.

Phone calls go unanswered. Forgive us.
Our mouths are full of tomatoes.
We are so busy
being small and hungry and alive.

New Fruit

When the words won't come,
I walk to the Asian mart up the road to fill
my blue basket with fruits I've never tried.
Prickly chom chom and sapodilla. Yellow pomelos
and mangosteen. Rose apples with their long sugar.
Often, I eat them unripe. I don't know better—lifting
each eager pome to the tongue, pulp between teeth.
I do it for the certain shock. To feel newness creep
into my body. A startling. The way your tongue
plunges into my mouth like a red knife. I want
to be tasted and skinned. Mouthed open and buoyant.
To be the pip inside your palm. This love, new
and crucial, a field—a dark belly for seeds.

In This New Life

There's a tree outside my window that taps the glass with her ancient hands. At night, I imagine her stroking my face. I chose this house because it has a fireplace to burn off bad days. In the sitting room, there's a built-in hutch—awkward as a stubbed toe. It's her ugliness that I love. I buy books and candles and thrift-store ramekins to line her shelves. If there are ghosts here, we are happy haunting one another. On Saturdays, I buy us all flowers. My cat snores on the bed. When I go out, I order French 75s because I've yet to hear anyone order one and not sound sexy. I wear a dress that doesn't hide my hips. In the tub, I listen to my grandfather's records. I'm naked and unrepentant. A fish with teeth. I've finally found a way to live on the inside of my life. This time, I'm the painter. This time, I'm the muse.

Culpable

I've always been haunted by choice. I want the city and the forest. Freedom but also babies. A home and the open highway.

I love it when other people choose anything for me—dinner spots, weekend plans, hiking trails. It's one tiny decision I'm absolved from making. To choose is to be culpable and as a former evangelical kid, there are few things I hate more than being *culpable*.

But being unable to choose becomes its own choice. When you don't decide, a decision still arrives.

Once I held the fleeting body of a farm cat newly struck on the side of a busy Ohio road. He'd gotten frightened in the rush and couldn't pick which way to go. So he stalled and was hit by the car in front of me. When I lifted the big body, shuddering and warm, I felt him die in my hands. Awful as it was, I listened to that heaviness. I knew it was a lesson. To decide is to survive.

I wrote a pep talk recently to myself on a bar napkin: *no matter which road you take, it will be both glorious and unbearable*. Every road is lonely. Every road, holy. The only error is not walking forth.

Yesterday, a friend in California, when giving me directions, told me I could take the trail toward the tall pines or turn left and find a field of poppies, growing gold and savage at the edge of the valley.

When I asked which to choose, she simply shrugged and said: *either way, it's all heaven*.

In Gratitude

Thank you brine of ocean,
tide that kept me restless.
Thank you sharp edge
of night, hot hands, smoke rage,
capsized schooner. Thank you seagulls
and sarcophagus, blood in sand. Thank you

stranger—and the solace of your palms.
Thank you road and detour, bruise and lipstick.
Thank you fire that would not start. Thank you
ash-dream and wet socks. Thank you wilderness, wave.

Whatever pitted me beneath the tide—
thank you. Brought me to the brink. Thank you
god by whatever name that would not let me drown.

Even If

Even if foolhardy,
ill-advised, or half-mad.
Even if you do not yet
understand your own
reasons and the waves
are at your throat. Even if
leaving guts your heart
to its last
thrumming fiber.
Even still, *go*
and let this life eat you
to the bone.

Acknowledgments

From the bottom of my heart, thank you to my first readers—
Jennifer Downey and Nellie Smith. And to my mother, who
inspired many poems in this book and whose constant enthusiasm
kept me writing. With thanks also to Remy Lankenau who gave
me courage and tenderness when I needed it most.

I'm indebted to my agent, Joanna MacKenzie, and my editor,
Whitney Frick, for their terrific kindness and unwavering support.

And finally, much gratitude to my writing community, Sustenance,
whose love and encouragement buoyed me up as I finished this
book.

About the Author

JOY SULLIVAN received an MA in poetry from Miami University, and her work has been published in *Boxcar Poetry Review*, *River Heron Review*, and *Bracken* magazine, among many others. Sullivan has served as the poet-in-residence for the Wexner Center for the Arts and has guest-lectured in classrooms from Stanford to Florida International University. She is also the founder of Sustenance, a community designed to help writers revitalize and nourish their craft.

joysullivanpoet.com
Instagram: @joysullivanpoet
joysullivan.substack.com

About the Type

This book was set in Electra, a typeface designed for Linotype by W. A. Dwiggins, the renowned type designer (1880–1956). Electra is a fluid typeface, avoiding the contrasts of thick and thin strokes that are prevalent in most modern typefaces.